The Forward Book
of Poetry 1993

First published in Great Britain by
Forward Publishing · 5 Great Pulteney Street · London WIR 3DF
in association with
Sinclair-Stevenson, an imprint of Reed Consumer Books Ltd
Michelin House · 81 Fulham Road · London SW3 6RB
and Auckland, Melbourne, Singapore and Toronto

ISBN 1 85619 298 9 (paperback) 1992

Compilation copyright © Forward Publishing 1992
For copyright in individual poems see acknowledgements page 9
Foreword copyright © Stephen Spender 1992

Printed and bound in Great Britain by
Mid Wales Litho Ltd, Pontypool
and JW Arrowsmith Ltd, Bristol
Typeset by JW Arrowsmith Ltd, Bristol

A CIP catalogue reference for this book
is available at the British Library.

The Forward Book
of Poetry 1993

FORWARD PUBLISHING
LONDON

To Paul Sieghart, in memoriam

Preface

IN COMPILING the Forward Book of Poetry we have set out to
give the reader as wide a selection as possible of the best poetry
being written in Britain today. The contrasting styles and
subjects mean that few will find all the works included in this
anthology to their taste, but I hope everyone will find
something they like and with their appetites whetted want to
find some more.

I often hear people saying that poetry is too difficult, too hard
to penetrate and understand. Like all art forms poetry is about
human expression. And part of what makes it so special to me is
its concision and musicality. Rhythm and cadence play a rich
role in verse and add to the meaning of the words themselves. I
can only counsel new readers of poetry to try reading it out
aloud and often. Layers of meaning and resonance will uncover
themselves on each rendition. But most of all a poem can
provide us with a vocabulary of expression, whether about love
or death, giving or grieving, which we cannot easily reach for
ourselves. Poetry can be a companion and a consolation; I hope
this anthology will become both to many.

In order to have established both the Forward Prize and this
anthology I have received considerable help and encouragement.
In particular I would like to thank Barnaby Rogerson for the
inspiration, Ed Victor for helping make it happen, Christine
Shaw of the Book Trust who actually made it happen and Kevin
Gavaghan of Midland Bank and Nicholas Wood of ABSA for
providing much of the funding. I would also like to thank, in
no particular order: Tim Waterstone, John Mitchinson,
Martyn Goff, Caroline Kay, Chris Rushby, Martin Lee, Chris
Green, Martha Smart, Jeffery Tolman, Julian Rivers,
Christopher Sinclair-Stevenson, Angela Martin, Dotti Irving,
Russell Taylor, Matthew Evans, Emma Mahony, Victoria
Cripps, Jo Abson, Rebecca Cripps and Lara Ivanovic for her
wonderful design.

Most of all thank you to our judges: Sir Stephen Spender, Margaret Drabble, Roger McGough, John Bayley and Mick Imlah, who have selected both our worthy prize winners and the poems that make up this anthology.

William Sieghart

Foreword

AFTER READING over two hundred poems we, the judges – John Bayley, Roger McGough, Margaret Drabble, Mick Imlah and myself – met to decide on the prize-winners, and also to choose poems for the accompanying anthology. After much debate, we decided that the prize-winners would be: Thom Gunn (first prize, £10,000); Simon Armitage (second prize, £5,000, for the most promising runner-up); and Jackie Kay, (third prize, £1,000, for her strikingly original poems).

Most of the time, of course, was spent in discussing the poems for the anthology. These had already to some extent been pre-selected for us by various organisations which had already given them prizes; some poems were recommended by editors of magazines.

Although there were several amateurish efforts submitted by what seem to be Poets' Mutual Admiration societies, on the whole the standard was remarkably high.

For better or worse (I am not quite sure which) a good many gifted people seem to be able to make poems out of the daily events in their lives. In their writing, these events are often interesting and nearly always to the point. What is encouraging is the feeling they give that these writers consider no subjects, no imagery, no vocabulary, is barred from poetry.

One can only rejoice that poets feel that poetry can be made out of many things and does not have to be about poetic subjects. There is, though, a danger attaching to this view: it is that if poetry can be about anything, anything can be poetry. Reading many of the poems submitted – even quite distinguished ones – the reader might well feel: 'Would not this be just as good in prose?' In awarding the prizes I think we were very conscious of feeling that a poem must be a verbal artefact which in form, vocabulary, texture, rhythm, must be distinct from some possibly alternative version which would be in prose.

Many of the poems which we chose for the anthology maintained this distinction. On the whole we felt that England may be on the verge of a revival of interest in poetry – both in the writing and the reading of it. A great many people reading poetry may, in a sense, be healthier for poetry than a great many people writing it.

Here we have chosen the best we could find, in the expectation that this anthology will find many readers.

Stephen Spender

Acknowledgements

Peter Abbs · THE MESSIAH · Western Mail International Poetry
   Competition 1991

Simon Armitage · POEM, BRASSNECK, GOOSEBERRY SEASON · *Kid*
   · Faber and Faber

George Barker · ON A BIRD DEAD IN THE ROAD · *Street Ballads*
   · Faber and Faber

Elizabeth Bartlett · ENTERING LANGUAGE · Winner, Staple Open Poetry
   Competition 1990

Michael Blackburn · ONE MORE · *The Prophecy of Christos* · Jackson's Arm

Rosita Boland · WOMAN AND THE KNIFE THROWER · *Muscle Creek*
   · Raven Arts Press

John Burnside · SEPTUAGESIMA · *Feast Days* · Secker & Warburg

Philip Casey · AND SO IT CONTINUES · *The Year of the Knife*
   · Raven Arts Press

Gladys Mary Coles · THE DORNIER · Winner, Aberystwyth Open Poetry
   Competition 1991 · Headland

David Constantine · THE PITMAN'S GARDEN · *Selected Poems*
   · Bloodaxe Books

Wendy Cope · TWO CURES FOR LOVE · *Serious Concerns* · Faber and Faber

Robert Crawford · GLASGOW 1989 · *Talkies* · Chatto & Windus

Iain Crichton Smith · THOSE · *Collected Poems* · Carcanet

Neil Curry · SKULLS · *Walking to Santiago* · Enitharmon

Tony Curtis · AT THE BORDER · *Poetry Wales* · Seren Books

Peter Dale · GOLDENROD · *Earthlight* · Hippopotamus Press

Carol Ann Duffy · ADULTERY · *Times Literary Supplement*

Ian Duhig · MARGIN PRAYER FROM AN ANCIENT PSALTER · *The Bradford
   Count* · Bloodaxe Books

Helen Dunmore · WHEN YOU'VE GOT · *The New Statesman*
   · Bloodaxe Books

G F Dutton · OPEN CAST · *The Concrete Garden* · Bloodaxe Books

U A Fanthorpe · DESCENT · *Neck-Verse* · Peterloo Poets

Tony Flynn · FATHER MICHAEL'S WAKING DREAM · *Body Politic*
· Bloodaxe Books

Mark Ford · A SWIMMING POOL FULL OF PEANUTS · *Landlocked*
· Chatto & Windus

Linda France · IF LOVE WAS JAZZ · *Red* · Bloodaxe Books

Elizabeth Garrett · FIRST LIGHT · *The Rule of Three* · Bloodaxe Books

Thom Gunn · LAMENT, DEATH'S DOOR, CAFETERIA IN BOSTON · *The Man
with Night Sweats* · Faber and Faber

Michael Hamburger · LIFE & ART IV · *Roots in the Air*
· Anvil Press Poetry

Tony Harrison · A COLD COMING · *A Cold Coming* · Bloodaxe Books

Linton Kwesi Johnson · MI REVALUESHANARY FREN · *Tings an Times*
· Bloodaxe Books

Jackie Kay · BLACK BOTTOM · *The Adoption Papers* · Bloodaxe Books

Alice Keen · A GREYHOUND IN THE EVENING AFTER A LONG DAY OF RAIN
· *Planet* · The Welsh Internationalist

Mimi Khalvati · STONE OF PATIENCE · *In White Ink* · Carcanet

Michael Laskey · A LATE WEDDING ANNIVERSARY POEM · *Thinking of
Happiness* · Peterloo Poets

John Levett · A SHRUNKEN HEAD · Joint winner, Poetry Society National
Poetry Competition 1991

David Lightfoot · TURNING POINT · *Down Private Lanes* · Winner,
Rosemary Arthur Award 1991 · National Poetry Foundation
Publications

Michael Longley · DETOUR · *Gorse Fires* · Winner, Whitbread Poetry
Award 1991 · Secker & Warburg

Lachlan MacKinnon · THE SINGLE LIFE · *The Coast of Bohemia*
· Chatto & Windus

Mary Maher · BY-PASS · *Snowfruit* · TAXUS at Stride

Glyn Maxwell · WE BILLION CHEERED · *Out of the Rain*
· Bloodaxe Books

Medbh McGuckian · A DIFFERENT SAME · *Marconi's Cottage*
· Bloodaxe Books

Jamie McKendrick · IL TREMOTO · *Times Literary Supplement* · Oxford
University Press

Ian McMillan · SNAILS ON THE WEST SHORE, AUGUST 1991 · Winner of
the BBC Wildlife Poet of the Year Award 1992

Patrick Moran · IN MEMORY OF FRANK NEVILLE · *The Honest Ulsterman*
· The Honest Ulsterman

David Morley · OZYMANDIAS To You · *Mandelstam Variations*
· Littlewood Arc

Thom Nairn · A QUIET BUSINESS · *Understanding Magazine*
· Dionysia Press

Sean O'Brien · PROPAGANDA · *HMS Glasshouse* · Oxford University Press

Bernard O'Donoghue · A NUN TAKES THE VEIL · *The Weakness*
· Chatto & Windus

Michael O'Neill · LOST · *London Magazine*

Evangeline Paterson · LUCIFER AT THE FAIR · *Lucifer At The Fair*
· TAXUS at Stride

Pauline Plummer · UNCLES AND AUNTIES · Winner, Tees Valley
Writer 1991

Peter Porter · WITTGENSTEIN's DREAM · *The Chair of Babel*
· Oxford University Press

Peter Reading · *from* EVAGATORY · *Evagatory* · Chatto & Windus

Christopher Reid · AMPHIBIOLOGY · *In The Echoey Tunnel*
· Faber and Faber

Mark Roper · SKINDEEP · *The Hen Ark* · Peterloo Poets/Salmon
Publishing · Winner, Aldeburgh Poetry Festival Prize 1991

William Scammell · THE EMPEROR OF CHINA · *Bleeding Heart Yard*
· Peterloo Poets

Jo Shapcott · PHRASE BOOK · Joint winner, The Poetry Society National
Poetry Competition 1991

Jon Silkin · URBAN GRASSES · *The Lens-Breakers* · Sinclair-Stevenson

Harry Smart · FLORINS · *Pierrot* · Faber and Faber

Contents

The Winning Poems

Thom Gunn

Your dying was a difficult enterprise.
First, petty things took up your energies,
The small but clustering duties of the sick,
Irritant as the cough's dry rhetoric.
Those hours of waiting for pills, shot, X-ray
Or test (while you read novels two a day)
Already with a kind of clumsy stealth
Distanced you from the habits of your health.
  In hope still, courteous still, but tired and thin,
You tried to stay the man that you had been,
Treating each symptom as a mere mishap
Without import. But then the spinal tap.
It brought a hard headache, and when night came
I heard you wake up from the same bad dream
Every half-hour with the same short cry
Of mild outrage, before immediately
Slipping into the nightmare once again
Empty of content but the drip of pain.
No respite followed: though the nightmare ceased,
Your cough grew thick and rich, its strength increased.
Four nights, and on the fifth we drove you down
To the Emergency Room. That frown, that frown:
I'd never seen such rage in you before
As when they wheeled you through the swinging door.
For you knew, rightly, they conveyed you from
Those normal pleasures of the sun's kingdom
The hedonistic body basks within
And takes for granted – summer on the skin,
Sleep without break, the moderate taste of tea
In a dry mouth. You had gone on from me
As if your body sought out martyrdom
In the far Canada of a hospital room.
Once there, you entered fully the distress

And long pale rigours of the wilderness.
A gust of morphine hid you. Back in sight
You breathed through a segmented tube, fat, white,
Jammed down your throat so that you could not speak.
    How thin the distance made you. In your cheek
One day, appeared the true shape of your bone
No longer padded. Still your mind, alone,
Explored this emptying intermediate
State for what holds and rests were hidden in it.
    You wrote us messages on a pad, amused
At one time that you had your nurse confused
Who, seeing you reconciled after four years
With your grey father, both of you in tears,
Asked if this was at last your 'special friend'
(The one you waited for until the end).
'She sings,' you wrote, 'a Philippine folk song
To wake me in the morning... It is long
And very pretty.' Grabbing at detail
To furnish this bare ledge toured by the gale,
On which you lay, bed restful as a knife,
You tried, tried hard, to make of it a life
Thick with the complicating circumstance
Your thoughts might fasten on. It had been chance
Always till now that had filled up the moment
With live specifics your hilarious comment
Discovered as it went along; and fed,
Laconic, quick, wherever it was led.
You improvised upon your own delight.
I think back to the scented summer night
We talked between our sleeping bags, below
A molten field of stars five years ago:
I was so tickled by your mind's light touch
I couldn't sleep, you made me laugh too much,
Though I was tired and begged you to leave off.

Now you were tired, and yet not tired enough
– Still hungry for the great world you were losing
Steadily in no season of your choosing –

And when at last the whole death was assured,
Drugs having failed, and when you had endured
Two weeks of an abominable constraint,
You faced it equably, without complaint,
Unwhimpering, but not at peace with it.
You'd lived as if your time was infinite:
You were not ready and not reconciled,
Feeling as uncompleted as a child
Till you had shown the world what you could do
In some ambitious role to be worked through,
A role your need for it had half-defined,
But never wholly, even in your mind.
You lacked the necessary ruthlessness,
The soaring meanness that pinpoints success.
We loved that lack of self-love, and your smile,
Rueful, at your own silliness.
                                        Meanwhile,
Your lungs collapsed, and the machine, unstrained,
Did all your breathing now. Nothing remained
But death by drowning on an inland sea
Of your own fluids, which it seemed could be
Kindly forestalled by drugs. Both could and would:
Nothing was said, everything understood,
At least by us. Your own concerns were not
Long-term, precisely, when they gave the shot
– You made local arrangements to the bed
And pulled a pillow round beside your head.
   And so you slept, and died, your skin gone grey,
Achieving your completeness, in a way.

Outdoors next day, I was dizzy from a sense
Of being ejected with some violence
From vigil in a white and distant spot
Where I was numb, into this garden plot
Too warm, too close, and not enough like pain.
I was delivered into time again
– The variations that I live among
Where your long body too used to belong

And where the still bush is minutely active.
You never thought your body was attractive,
Though others did, and yet you trusted it
And must have loved its fickleness a bit
Since it was yours and gave you what it could,
Till near the end it let you down for good,
Its blood hospitable to those guests who
Took over by betraying it into
The greatest of its inconsistencies
This difficult, tedious, painful enterprise.

DEATH'S DOOR

Of course the dead outnumber us
– How their recruiting armies grow!
My mother archaic now as Minos,
She who died forty years ago.

After their processing, the dead
Sit down in groups and watch TV,
In which they must be interested,
For on it they see you and me.

These four, who though they never met
Died in one month, sit side by side
Together in front of the same set,
And all without a *TV Guide*.

Arms round each other's shoulders loosely,
Although they can feel nothing, who
When they unlearned their pain so sprucely
Let go of all sensation too.

Thus they watch friend and relative
And life here as they think it is
– In black and white, repetitive
As situation comedies.

With both delight and tears at first
They greet each programme on death's stations,
But in the end lose interest,
Their boredom turning to impatience.

'He misses me? He must be kidding
– This week he's sleeping with a cop.'
'All she reads now is *Little Gidding*.'
'They're getting old. I wish they'd stop.'

The habit of companionship
Lapses – they break themselves of touch:
Edging apart at arm and hip,
Till separated on the couch,

They woo amnesia, look away
As if they were not yet elsewhere,
And when snow blurs the picture they,
Turned, give it a belonging stare.

Snow blows out toward them, till their seat
Filling with flakes becomes instead
Snow-bank, snow-landscape, and in that
They find themselves with all the dead,

Where passive light from snow-crust shows them
Both Minos circling and my mother.
Yet none of the recruits now knows them,
Nor do they recognize each other,

They have been so superbly trained
Into the perfect discipline
Of an archaic host, and weaned
From memory briefly barracked in.

CAFETERIA IN BOSTON

I could digest the white slick watery mash,
The two green peppers stuffed with rice and grease
In Harry's Cafeteria, could digest
Angelfood cake too like a sweetened sawdust.
I sought to extend the body's education,
Forced it to swallow down the blunted dazzle
Sucked from the red formica where I leaned.
Took myself farther, digesting as I went,
Course after course: even the bloated man
In cast-off janitor's overalls, who may
Indeed have strayed through only for the toilets;
But as he left I caught his hang-dog stare
At the abandoned platefuls crusted stiff
Like poisoned slugs that froth into their trails.
I stomached him, him of the flabby stomach,
Though it was getting harder to keep down.
But how about the creature scurrying in
From the crowds wet on the November sidewalk,
His face a black skull with a slaty shine,
Who slipped his body with one fluid motion
Into a seat before a dish on which
Scrapings had built a heterogeneous mound,
And set about transferring them to his mouth,
Stacking them faster there than he could swallow,
To get a start on the bus-boys. My mouth too
Was packed, its tastes confused: what bitter juices
I generated in my stomach as
Revulsion met revulsion. Yet at last
I lighted upon meat more to my taste

When, glancing off into the wide fluorescence,
I saw the register, where the owner sat,
And suddenly realized that he, the cooks,
The servers of the line, the bus-boys, all
Kept their eyes studiously turned away
From the black scavenger. Digestively,
That was the course that kept the others down.

Simon Armitage

POEM

And if it snowed and snow covered the drive
he took a spade and tossed it to one side.
And always tucked his daughter up at night.
And slippered her the one time that she lied.

And every week he tipped up half his wage.
And what he didn't spend each week he saved.
And praised his wife for every meal she made.
And once, for laughing, punched her in the face.

And for his mum he hired a private nurse.
And every Sunday taxied her to church.
And he blubbed when she went from bad to worse.
And twice he lifted ten quid from her purse.

Here's how they rated him when they looked back:
sometimes he did this, sometimes he did that.

BRASSNECK

United, mainly,
every odd Saturday,
or White Hart Lane for a worthwhile away game.
Down in the crowds at the grounds where the bread is:
the gold, the plastic,
the cheque-books, the readies,

the biggest fish
or the easiest meat,
or both. Consider that chap we took last week:
we turned him over and walked off the terrace
with a grand exactly
in dog-eared tenners;

takings like that
don't get reported.
Carter, he's a sort of junior partner;
it's two seasons now since we first teamed up
in the Stretford End
in the FA Cup;

it was all United
when I caught him filching
my cigarette case, and he felt me fishing
a prial of credit cards out of his britches.
Since that day
we've worked these pitches.

We tend to kick off
by the hot dog vans
and we've lightened a good many fair-weather fans
who haven't a clue where to queue for tickets.
Anything goes, if it's
loose we lift it.

At City last year
in the derby match
we did the right thing with a smart-looking lass
who'd come unhitched in the crush from her friend.
We escorted her out
of the Platt Lane End,

arm in arm
along the touchline,
past the tunnel and out through the turnstile
and directed her on to a distant police car.
I did the talking
and Carter fleeced her.

As Carter once put it:
when we're on the ball
we can clean someone out, from a comb to a coil,
and we need nine eyes to watch for the coppers
though at Goodison Park
when I got collared

two bright young bobbies
took me into the toilets
and we split the difference. Bent policemen;
there's always a couple around when you need them.
It's usually Autumn
when we loosen our fingers

at the Charity Shield
which is pretty big business
though semis and finals are birthdays and Christmas.
Hillsborough was a different ball game of course;
we'd started early,
then saw what the score was,

so we turned things in
as a mark of respect,
just kept enough back to meet certain expenses
(I'm referring here to a red and blue wreath;
there are trading standards,
even among thieves).

Carter keeps saying
he'd be quick to wager
that worse things go on in the name of wages,
but I've let Carter know there's a place and a time
to say as we speak,
speak as we find.

Speaking of Carter,
and not that I mind,
he thinks I'm a touch on the gingery side:
my voice a little too tongued and grooved,
my locks a little
too washed and groomed,

my cuticles tenderly
pushed back and pruned,
both thumbnails capped with a full half-moon,
each fingernail manicured, pared and polished...
We can work hand in hand if we stick to the rules:
he keeps his cunt-hooks out of my wallet,
I keep my tentacles
out of his pocket.

GOOSEBERRY SEASON

Which reminds me. He appeared
at noon, asking for water. He'd walked from town
after losing his job, leaving a note for his wife and his brother
and locking his dog in the coal bunker.
We made him a bed

and he slept till Monday.
A week went by and he hung up his coat.
Then a month, and not a stroke of work, a word of thanks,
a farthing of rent or a sign of him leaving.
One evening he mentioned a recipe

for smooth, seedless gooseberry sorbet
but by then I was tired of him: taking pocket money
from my boy at cards, sucking up to my wife and on his last night
sizing up my daughter. He was smoking my pipe
as we stirred his supper.

Where does the hand become the wrist?
Where does the neck become the shoulder? The watershed
and then the weight, whatever turns up and tips us over that
    razor's edge
between something and nothing, between
one and the other.

I could have told him this
but didn't bother. We ran him a bath
and held him under, dried him off and dressed him
and loaded him into the back of the pick-up.
Then we drove without headlights
to the county boundary,

dropped the tailgate, and after my boy
had been through his pockets we dragged him like a mattress
across the meadow and on the count of four
threw him over the border.

This is not general knowledge, except
in gooseberry season, which reminds me, and at the table
I have been known to raise an eyebrow, or scoop the sorbet
into five equal portions, for the hell of it.
I mention this for a good reason.

Jackie Kay

Chapter 7: Black Bottom

Maybe that's why I don't like
all this talk about her being black,
I brought her up as my own
as I would any other child
colour matters to the nutters;
but she says my daughter says
it matters to her

I suppose there would have been things
I couldn't understand with any child,
we knew she was coloured.
They told us they had no babies at first
and I chanced it didn't matter what colour it was
and they said *oh well are you sure*
in that case we have a baby for you –
to think she wasn't even thought of as a baby,
my baby, my baby

I chase his *Sambo Sambo* all the way from the school gate.
A fistful of anorak – What did you call me? Say that again.
Sam-bo . He plays the word like a bouncing ball
but his eyes move fast as ping pong.
I shove him up against the wall,
say that again you wee shite. *Sambo, sambo*, he's crying now

I knee him in the balls. What was that?
My fist is steel; I punch and punch his gut.
Sorry I didn't hear you? His tears drip like wax.
Nothing he heaves *I didn't say nothing*.
I let him go. He is a rat running. He turns
and shouts *Dirty Darkie* I chase him again.
Blonde hairs in my hand. Excuse me!
This teacher from primary 7 stops us.
Names? I'll report you to the headmaster tomorrow.
But Miss. Save it for Mr Thompson she says

My teacher's face cracks into a thin smile
Her long nails scratch the note well well
I see you were fighting yesterday, again.
In a few years time you'll be a juvenile delinquent.
Do you know what that is? Look it up in the dictionary.
She spells each letter with slow pleasure.
Read it out to the class.
Thug. Vandal. Hooligan. Speak up. Have you lost your tongue?

To be honest I hardly ever think about it
except if something happens, you know
daft talk about darkies. Racialism.
Mothers ringing my bell with their kids
crying *You tell. You tell. You tell.*
– *No.* You tell your little girl to stop calling
my little girl names and I'll tell my little girl
to stop giving your little girl a doing.

We're practising for the school show
I'm trying to do the Cha Cha and the Black Bottom
but I can't get the steps right
my right foot's left and my left foot's right
my teacher shouts from the bottom
of the class Come on, show

us what you can do I thought
you people had it in your blood.
My skin is hot as burning coal
like that time she said Darkies are like coal
in front of the whole class – my blood
what does she mean? I thought

she'd stopped all that after the last time
my dad talked to her on parents' night
the other kids are all right till she starts;
my feet step out of time, my heart starts
to miss beats like when I can't sleep at night –
What Is In My Blood? The bell rings, it is time.

Sometimes it is hard to know what to say
that will comfort. Us two in the armchair;
me holding her breath, 'they're ignorant
let's have some tea and cake, forget them'.

Maybe it's really Bette Davis I want
to be the good twin or even better the bad
one or a nanny who drowns a baby in a bath.
I'm not sure maybe I'd prefer Katharine
Hepburn tossing my red hair, having a hot
temper. I says to my teacher Can't I be
Elizabeth Taylor, drunk and fat and she
just laughed, not much chance of that.
I went for an audition for the *The Prime*
of Miss Jean Brodie. I didn't get a part
even though I've been acting longer
than Beverley Innes. So I have. Honest.

Olubayo was the colour of peat
when we walked out heads turned
like horses, folk stood like trees
their eyes fixed on us – it made me
burn, that hot glare; my hand
would sweat down to his bone.
Finally, alone, we'd melt
nothing, nothing would matter

He never saw her. I looked for him in her;
for a second it was as if he was there
in that glass cot looking back through her.

On my bedroom wall is a big poster
of Angela Davis who is in prison
right now for nothing at all
except she wouldn't put up with stuff.
My mum says she is *only* 26
which seems really old to me
but my mum says it is young
just imagine, she says, being on
America's Ten Most Wanted People's List at 26!
I can't.
Angela Davis is the only female person
I've seen (except for a nurse on TV)
who looks like me. She had big hair like mine
that grows out instead of down.
My mum says it's called an *Afro*.
If I could be as brave as her when I get older
I'll be OK.

Last night I kissed her goodnight again
and wondered if she could feel the kisses
in prison all the way from Scotland.
Her skin is the same too you know.
I can see my skin is that colour
but most of the time I forget,
so sometimes when I look in the mirror
I give myself a bit of a shock
and say to myself *Do you really look like this?*
as if I'm somebody else. I wonder if she does that.

I don't believe she killed anybody.
It is all a load of phoney lies.
My dad says it's a set up.
I asked him if she'll get the electric chair
like them Roseberries he was telling me about.
No he says the world is on her side.
Well how come she's in there then I thinks.
I worry she's going to get the chair.
I worry she's worrying about the chair.
My dad says she'll be putting on a brave face.
He brought me a badge home which I wore
to school. It says FREE ANGELA DAVIS.
And all my pals says 'Who's she?'

Other Poems

Peter Abbs

THE MESSIAH

We had been waiting ever since we were born,
Crouched in the kitchen, where the ceiling flaked,
Or in the parlour with the curtains drawn –

As if home was the birth-place for a dread
That defied naming. The monologue of fear
Was in our eyes. Little was ever said.

Then as Spring was about to break each year,
A tall man arrived with a chalice of ash.
Thou art dust, he chanted in my ear,

And unto dust thou shalt return. With his thumb
He pressed the crumbling mark of Christ
Into our baffled flesh. My mind went numb.

We spent our lives with our knees on marble
In obscure corners with confessional voices
Heard just out of reach. Yet I was more than sure

We would be notified when the event came,
Receive an official letter giving a date
And a place, a number and a name.

Yet He arrived unannounced. A knock on the door
On another uneventful day and the Messiah
Stood there, smooth-shaved and assured.

He told us to leave things as they were.
We nodded. And assembled like Jews.
The kettle steamed into the air,

The dogs yelped and scratched at the door.
We lined up like cherubim.
It was the end we had been waiting for.

George Barker

On a Bird Dead in the Road

What formerly flounced and flew its fantastic feathers
Now lies like a flattened old leather glove in the road,
And the gigantic wheels of the articulated juggernaut lorries
Pound down on it all day long like the mad will of god.

Elizabeth Bartlett

ENTERING LANGUAGE

Mothers remember the first word,
rising like a stone in a stream
of babbling. I hear the word *dot*
from my miniature pointillist
unsteady in his painted cot.
The first snow, and *Dots, dots, dots*
he cries with the eloquence and tone
of a lay preacher spreading the word
to a deaf world. We are as ecstatic
and amazed as Seurat discovering
the phenomena of vision. In his world
of wooden bars and hemispheres
of milky white, dots surround us
for a few days, stars are pin-heads
at night, sugar glacial specks;
we dot and carry one, hear Morse code
in our sleep, wake on the dot of six.
There's no doubt we are all dotty,
but soon we are into language,
no pause each day for breath;
linked words, sentences gather momentum.
Dots all gone away, he greets the sun.
We welcome him into our world; he picks
out commas, colons and full-stops
to please us, but Os are more exciting.
Oh, we cry to everything, but it palls
at last; the Great Os of Advent
turn into yawns. At dawn we hear him
trying out the seven antiphons and groan.

Michael Blackburn

ONE MORE

one more rush of wind on a crowded platform,
one more drunk asleep on a bench,
one more nutter with a blitzed brain screaming,
one more smashed-up telephone, one more night of sirens,
one more ruck of skins shouting *kill the niggers*,
one more stranger's malevolent stare,
one more room at a criminal rent, one more landlord
trying it on, one more late train not arriving,
one more barman passing short change, one more
middle-class pig pushing in with his girlfriend,
one more pimp giving a Soho wink, one more pervert
buying in flashcubes, one more corpse for the river police,
one more trip to the social, one more time

Rosita Boland

THE WOMAN AND THE KNIFE-THROWER

I am the woman whom the knife-thrower
Redefines each night,
The knives flying surely
From his calloused palm.

I have no beauty, no humour,
No lithe and acrobatic skills
And so I have become a human prop
In this tawdry circus.

The knife-thrower
Knows the outlines of my body
As no other person does.

All day, he sits on the caravan steps
And polishes knives.
He watches me
In the reflection of their cruel blades.

Night after night,
I entrust my body to him.

We mark each other, eye to eye,
And the knives come like the words
He will never speak.

They brush against my flesh, glittering
With the brightness of unshed tears.

John Burnside

SEPTUAGESIMA

'Nombres.
Están sobre la pátina
  de las cosas.'
(Jorge Guillén)

I dream of the silence
the day before Adam came
to name the animals,

the gold skins newly dropped
from God's bright fingers, still
implicit with the light.

A day like this, perhaps:
a winter whiteness
haunting the creation,

as we are sometimes
haunted by the space
we fill, or by the forms

we might have known
before the names,
beyond the gloss of things.

Philip Casey

Beyond the headstones in the graveyard
there is a special plot for limbs.
Severed legs and arms
mingle promiscuously in death,
if they missed their chance in life.
The hand of someone's husband
rests on the leg of someone's wife.

Gladys Mary Coles

THE DORNIER

The moorland blazing and a bomber's moon
lit skies light as a June dawn,
the harvest stubble to a guilty flush.
I saw from the farmhouse the smoking plane
like a giant bat in a sideways dive,
fuel spewing from its underbelly.
I remember how one wing tipped our trees
tearing the screen of pines like lace,
flipping over, flimsy as my balsa models.
It shattered on the pasture, killing sheep,
ripping the fence where the shot fox hung.
Dad let me look next morning at the wreck –
it lay in two halves like a broken wasp,
nose nestled in the ground, blades
of the propellers bent...
I thought I saw them moving
in the wind.

If the Invader comes, the leaflet said,
Do not give a German anything. Do not tell him
anything. Hide your food and bicycles.
Hide your maps. ... But these Luftwaffe men
were dead. Their machine, a carcass
cordoned off. A museum dinosaur.
Don't go nearer. Do not touch.

Trophies, I took – a section of the tail
(our collie found it dangling in the hedge),
pieces of perspex like thin ice on the grass,
some swapped for shrapnel down at school
(how strangely it burned in a slow green flame).
Inscribed *September 1940, Nantglyn,*
the black-crossed relic now hangs on our wall.
My son lifts it down, asks questions
I can't answer.

Yesterday, turning the far meadow for new drains,
our blades hit three marrows, huge and hard,
stuffed with High Explosive – the Dornier's final gift.
Cordoned off, they're photographed, defused.
I take my son to see the empty crater,
the imprint of their shapes still in the soil –
shadows that turn up time.

David Constantine

THE PITMAN'S GARDEN
(For Bill and Diane Williamson)

Man called Teddy had a garden in
The ruins of Mary Magdalen
By Baxter's Scrap. Grew leeks. What leeks need is
Plenty of shite and sunshine. Sunshine's His
Who gave His only begotten Son to give
Or not but shite is up to us who live
On bread and meat and veg and every day
While Baxter fished along the motorway
For write-offs Teddy arrived with bags of it
From home, which knackered him, the pit
Having blacked his lungs. But Baxter towed in wrecks
On their hind-legs with dolls and busted specs
And things down backs of seats still in and pressed
Them into oxo cubes and Teddy addressed
His ranks of strapping lads and begged them grow
Bonnier and bonnier. Before the show
For fear of slashers he made his bed up there
Above the pubs, coughing on the night air,
Like the Good Shepherd Teddy lay
Under the stars, hearing the motorway,
Hearing perhaps the concentrated lives
Of family cars in Baxter's iron hives.
Heard Baxter's dog howl like a coyote
And sang to his leeks 'Nearer my God to Thee'.
He lays his bearded beauties out. Nothing
On him is so firm and white, but he can bring
These for a common broth and eat his portion.

Leaving town, heading for the M1,
Watch out for the pitman's little garden in
The ruined fold of Mary Magdalen.

Wendy Cope

TWO CURES FOR LOVE

1 Don't see him. Don't phone or write a letter.
2 The easy way: get to know him better.

Robert Crawford

Glasgow 1989
for Frank Kuppner

Wind souchs on the hot lawns of Kelvinbridge.
Back after ten years, a young Sikh stares at where tenements were
In the early evening, remembering
How he grew up under this grass.

In the newsagent's/gapsite/demolished warehouse
Janice is xeroxing copyright music,
Singing *Flower of Scotland*. That ex-
Railway bridge is just sky.

A sculpted paper boat, berg-sized,
Floats off berths zoned for redevelopment.
Wee Shuggy, Dave, and Wonderwoman
Hang around waiting for a zebra.

Iain Crichton Smith

THOSE

Those who are given early retirement and the radiant handshake
shuffle after their wives in crowded rooms;

following them like dogs as they used to follow ideas
over horizons which were once fresh and blue.

They come to rest in fields on which once rainbows
rested like bridges among summer flowers

but now the end is in sight, the box is open
with its sweet poisons of the merciless days

and the sought fragrances which never really appear.
The hoover bites at the legs, as at great windows

they look out at the sea where boats with names
like Dayspring and Diligence rock on their rusty chains.

Neil Curry

SKULLS
(For John Wood)

Down where the swash and backwash of the tide
Had retched up wet entanglements
Of bladder wrack and kelp, the usual
Goitred orange and a single shoe,
We found the dead gannet;

Its intricate, slim wings intact as when
We saw them fold like paper darts
And plunge into the seas round Boreray;
And still with that slight blush of yellow
To the head, like a girl's chin

When you hold a buttercup beneath it.
And I wanted that skull – the great beak
Longer than my longest finger – to put
Beside the hooked and sun-bleached hawk's
On my windowsill.

But lifting it I found the tongue gone
And a thick gruel of maggots
Already on the boil in its gullet.
And I couldn't touch it. We walked off
Talking of flowers instead:

Of the misty and paler-than-harebell blue
Of the sea holly, Crippen's henbane,
And the trumpets of convolvulus
Like the horns of ancient gramophones
Shaped out of porcelain.

But looking back I saw how the wind lifted
One wing and let it flap and fall
Like Ahab's arm when the white whale sounded,
Breached and rolled. And I thought of others
That I had missed out on:

Those oiled razorbills at St Bees,
The rat-gnawed heron on the banks
Of the Nene, and I knew that the only way
To win skulls such as those would have been
To take a knife to them,

Slicing into feather and skin, probing
For the vertebrae, to sever
Cartilage and ligament and cut through
To the bone. It's either that or waiting
For the sea's gift, or the sun's.

Tony Curtis

AT THE BORDER

When I tilt the can over the herb border
she's planted, no water comes.
I tilt again, but still nothing shows.
Leaves, I suppose, have clogged
the spout from last autumn, rotted and plugged
so the water's locked in.

With both hands I lift to eye level
the laden, awkward can and tip again.
This roadside gift fallen from a builder's truck,
battered and cement-stained, with no rose,
has been ours for three different gardens. It won't work,
and I am miming in that silent film
where the children have stepped on the hose.

I lower it and shake, until from the sharp funnel
emerges like a pencil lead the beak
and then the head of a bird.
I make the water force it halfway through
until the shoulders clear and it thrusts
like some bow-sprit figure from the spout.
It is absurd and saddening – its eyes shut,
a blind, futile arrow.

One of this spring's young, curious,
has flown into the can's nesting dark
where I left it safe under the sycamores
and, soft thing, after its flutter
in the echoing space has chosen
that jewel of light promised at the spout
before the easy freedom of the can's wide brim.

Pointing its way up the shaft of blue sky
this days-old starling
wormed its way into a coffin of light
which tightened and starved it in the mildest of springs.
Now, in the early summer sun, I lift the can once more
and force the bird in a shower of wet light
out and into the herb border.

Safe from the magpies and neighbours' cats
in the musk of rosemary and marjoram,
worked by the weather, bone and feather
will break down into soil that
feeds our parsley, chives and thyme.

Peter Dale

GOLDENROD

More is forgotten than remembered.
  I cannot tell you why it is I hate
  these goldenrod. I've always hated them,
and any goldenrod, by any gateway.
  One day when I am old, and the glossed light
  of childhood seems eternity too late,
it may come back to me in living spite,
  prompting some feeling for an hour or spasm–
  dull, yellow-dusted peaks of even height–
when, deaf to me, the feigned enthusiasm
  of your vague words that never had a season
  is painless as passing time, the trembling aspen;
and love's become as trivial as these
  stalks of goldenrod, well out of it,
  that I smash and enjoy smashing as I please
because they have their season, and they split
  cleanly, unlike the pliancy of trees.
–Now match your forceful mouth to this mad fit.

Carol Ann Duffy

ADULTERY

Wear dark glasses in the rain.
Regard what was unhurt
as though through a bruise.
Guilt. A sick, green tint.

New gloves, money tucked in the palms,
the handshake crackles. Hands
can do many things. Phone.
Open the wine. Wash themselves. Now

you are naked under your clothes all day,
slim with deceit. Only the once
brings you alone to your knees,
miming, more, more; older and sadder,

creative. Suck a lie with a hole in it
on the way home from a lethal, thrilling night
up against a wall, faster. Language
unpeels to a lost cry. You're a bastard.

Do it do it do it. Sweet darkness
in the afternoon; a voice in your ear
telling you how you are wanted,
which way, now. A telltale clock

wiping the hours from its face, your face
on a white sheet, gasping, radiant, yes.
Pay for it in cash, fiction, cab-fares back
to the life which crumbles like a wedding-cake.

Paranoia for lunch; too much
to drink, as a hand on your thigh
tilts the restaurant. You know all about love,
don't you. Turn on your beautiful eyes

for a stranger who's dynamite in bed, again
and again; a slow replay in the kitchen
where the slicing of innocent onions
scalds you to tears. Then, selfish autobiographical sleep

in a marital bed, the tarnished spoon of your body
stirring betrayal, your heart over-ripe at the core.
You're an expert, darling; your flowers
dumb and explicit on nobody's birthday.

So write the script – illness and debt,
a ring thrown away in a garden
no moon can heal, your own words
commuting to bile in your mouth, terror –

and all for the same thing twice. And all
for the same thing twice. You did it.
What. Didn't you. Fuck. Fuck. No. That was
the wrong verb. This is only an abstract noun.

Ian Duhig

MARGIN PRAYER FROM AN ANCIENT PSALTER

Lord I know, and I know you know I know
this is a drudge's penance. Only dull scholars
or cowherds maddened with cow-watching
will ever read *The Grey Psalter of Antrim*.
I have copied it these thirteen years
waiting for the good bits – High King of the Roads,
are there any good bits in *The Grey Psalter of Antrim*?

(Text illegible here because of teeth-marks.)

It has the magic realism of an argumentum:
it has the narrative subtlety of the Calendar of Oengus;
it has the oblique wit of the Battle-Cathach of the O'Donnells;
it grips like the colophon to The Book of Durrow;
it deconstructs like a canon-table;
it makes St Jerome's Defence of his Vulgate look racy.
I would make a gift of it to Halfdane the Sacker
that he might use it to wipe his wide Danish arse.
Better its volumes intincted our cattle-trough
and cured poor Luke, my three-legged calf,
than sour my wit and spoil my calligraphy.
Luke! White Luke! Truer beast than Ciarán's Dun Cow!
You would rattle the abbot with your soft off-beats
butting his churns and licking salt from his armpits.
Luke, they flayed you, pumiced your skin to a wafer –
such a hide as King Tadhg might die under –
for pages I colour with ox-gall yellow...

(Text illegible here because of tear-stains.)

Oh Forgiving Christ of scribes and sinners
intercede for me with the jobbing abbot!
Get me re-assigned to something pagan
with sex and perhaps gratuitous violence
which I might deplore with insular majuscule
and illustrate with Mozarabic complexity
Ad maioram gloriam Dei et Hiberniae,
and lest you think I judge the book too harshly
from pride or a precious sensibility
I have arranged for a second opinion.
Tomorrow our surveyor, Ronan the Barbarian,
will read out loud as only he can read out loud
selected passages from this which I have scored
while marking out his new church in Killaney
in earshot of that well-versed man, King Suibhne...

(Text completely illegible from this point
because of lake-water damage and otter dung.)

Helen Dunmore

WHEN YOU'VE GOT

When you've got the plan of your life
matched to the time it will take
but you just want to press SHIFT/BREAK
and print over and over
this is not what I was after
this is not what I was after,

when you've finally stripped out the house
with its iron-cold fireplace,
its mouldings, its mortgage,
its single-skin walls
but you want to write in the plaster
"This is not what I was after,"

when you've got the rainbow-clad baby
in his state-of-the-art pushchair
but he arches his back at you
and pulps his Activity Centre
and you just want to whisper
"This is not what I was after,"

when the vacuum seethes and whines in the lounge
and the waste-disposal unit blows,
when tenners settle in your account
like snow hitting a stove,
when you get a chat from your spouse
about marriage and personal growth,

when a wino comes to sleep in your porch
on your Citizen's Charter
and you know a hostel's opening soon
but your headache's closer
and you really just want to torch
the bundle of rags and newspaper

and you'll say to the newspaper
"This is not what we were after,
this is not what we were after."

G F Dutton

OPEN CAST

It will all be put back
just as it was before.

At present, my dear,
it may be a scar
an open wound, a hole in the ground

a quarter mile square:
that's nothing to fear –
we have mended, all round,

holes that were,
filled them in by the million ton
hammered them down

to hectares of beautiful green, each one
rolled out between – how far, how far –
high-tensile wire;

and simply alive
with mutton and beef.
You'd never believe

how solid they are, how safe
with the ashes tucked underneath.
And this hole here

will be as pretty a place –
you'll recognise
the lane, the flowers, the trees

the field with the blue butterflies. And yes
you will love her as much as your mother, so please
don't cry any more.

It will all be put back
just as it was before.

U A Fanthorpe

DESCENT

Some unremembered ancestor handed down to me
The practice of walking in darkness.

I didn't ask for it. I didn't want it.
Would choose to be without, if choice could move

The hard *fiat* of genes. I don't like darkness,
Its arbitrary swoops of stairs, its tunnel vaults,

Black bristly air, its emptiness. Others speak
Of the shining end of the tunnel. I haven't seen it.

This is my black. I alone
Am the authority, and I know no further

Than I've got, if that be anywhere.
I inherited no maps. A feckless line.

So I choose you, intransigent old Roman,
As ancestor; who, at the City's

Most sinister hour, fathomed the riddle;
Who faced the *it*; who, a man in arms and mounted,

Willingly entered the dark; who worked, however blindly,
However strangely, for good, under the earth. Who worked.

*'Old Roman': Mettus Curtius. In BC 362 the earth in the Roman
forum gave way. A chasm appeared, and soothsayers said it could only
be filled by throwing in the city's greatest treasure. Mettus Curtius
armed himself, mounted his horse, and leaped in. The earth closed over
him.*

Tony Flynn

FATHER MICHAEL'S WAKING DREAM

She calls to him now
from the edge of the pool –

Bless me,
Father, for I have
sinned...

Laughing, she
steps from her thin
blue dress –

        ...sticky
red leaves
in your matted hair, O
my sweet, my
precious one...

and turns from the trees
towards him.
        His vision
swims and blurs.

He blinks –

The black dog sprawled
across her shadow, nosing her grassy
cleft, might be his cassock
sloughed on the lawn,

or his own shadow
darker on hers.

Mark Ford

A SWIMMING-POOL FULL OF PEANUTS

A stifling blanket day out west I was working the desert states
nothing for days thank-you ma'm door slams in my face (again)
so I mosey out round the back where my vehicle sits melting I'll
just check the set-up the outhouses the grass is all stiff
and plastic the trees are all lifeless and there's no shade
nothing stirring until I come across right in the open
a whole swimming-pool full of peanuts I think
I've gone mad so I shut my eyes and I count
to five and look again and they're still resting there
very quietly an inch or so I suppose below
the high-water mark they're a light tan colour
and the tiles around are a lovely cool aqua-blue
only there's no water just these peanuts.
Well this is a hoax I can tell some monkey's idea
of a good joke for who'd fill up a fair-sized swimming-
pool entirely with peanuts unless they're painted in
which case it's a nice piece of work so I
kneel down in my best suit on the edge
(tie at half-mast because of the heat)
and with a loud snigger I dip in my finger
just to see it sinks into small grainy nuggets
sand-coated and a bit greasy some whole some in
half I draw it out and examine it all shiny with oil
the nail gleaming and I lick it to find out the taste
SALT! madness! the genuine article! straight salted peanuts!
this gets me because what kind of mad case goes
to the trouble of building a swimming-pool and then fills it
instead of with water with salted peanuts right up to the brim
I'm the butt of his jest this goop is taking the michael
almost physically I can feel him pulling my leg so
I lean over again and lower my head carefully until my
left eye is level with the glistening expanse for no
reason I'm feeling all queasy this pool full of peanuts

is disturbing my eye won't focus in case in an instant
they turn into piranha fish and green mambas
or anything else that might be hiding down there.

Still nothing moved I admit it was quiet too quiet
all I could hear was my own labouring breath
so in both clammy hands I scoop up fistful after fistful
and I watch them trickle through my fingers and glitter in
the sun I go back to my car and open up the trunk
I take out my golf-bag I select a nine-iron
and without a thought for my own safety I head back
to the pool and I swing away reckless in that peanut bunker
I scatter peanuts like a madman all over around there
they go flying like sand-flies in all directions like golf-
balls they arc away and shower down like buff-coloured hail
and I thresh and flail like one possessed
but nothing is uncovered it's no good from the edge
so feet first I leap in at the deep end
brandishing my golf-club and hit away
like a good soldier but there's more and more always
though I swing a good hour at the end of that
I am exhausted and my skin itches from the salt
and my clothes are all clinging I collapse in the middle
buoyed up by the peanuts the whole thing is hopeless
my pores are all clogged so I say let sleeping dogs lie
and I crawl to the side and haul myself out and
shake out the loose peanuts from the creases of my suit
I pick them out of my socks and empty out my shoes
I brush them out of my armpits and angrily I throw
my nine-iron into the middle of the pool where it sinks
without trace and I storm back to my car and
I make this resolution never ever if you can ever avoid it
fool around with a swimming-pool like this one
well a swimming-pool full of peanuts is not worth the trouble.

Linda France

If Love Was Jazz

If love was jazz,
I'd be dazzled
By its razzmatazz.

If love was a sax
I'd melt in its brassy flame
Like wax.

If love was a guitar,
I'd pluck its six strings,
Eight to the bar.

If love was a trombone,
I'd feel its slow
Slide, right down my backbone.

If love was a drum,
I'd be caught in its snare,
Kept under its thumb.

If love was a trumpet,
I'd blow it.

If love was jazz,
I'd sing its praises,
Like Larkin has.

But love isn't jazz.
It's an organ recital.
Eminently worthy,
Not nearly as vital.

If love was jazz,
I'd always want more.
I'd be a regular
On that smoky dance-floor.

Elizabeth Garrett

FIRST LIGHT
from a sequence of poems called 'RUMAUCOURT'

When first we woke in that place, we may have sensed
Our own desertion there,
Lying in the high room, in the too high bed,
Searching the light as it edged on the window-sill
Too slowly, and eight flies in aimless quadrille
Troubled the tall air.

At cock-crow, memory crept back like a truant lover
Mocking our wise fear
Of the stiff furniture, the dust cover
Of sleep, till we longed to abandon what we'd become
Beneath sleep in that strange bed and abandoned room
Waiting for light to appear.

We are ourselves and more, waking to what
We've come for; finding more
Than we want or can ever push back, like the slow light
On the window-sill, the heavy sheets, the air,
The importunate tug of the blood, our being here
Waking to Rumaucourt.

Michael Hamburger

But what rose, Gertrude Stein?
The rose you verbalized was never mine.
Nor is a rose a rose
Till definite by place and kind it grows.
Your triple 'a' rose without shape and colour
Permutes to nothingness, at each turn duller.
I left a hedgerow dog-rose, white and light,
Anyone's flower. The tea-rose in this park,
Though public before dark,
Is no one's when through bars it fades from sight
Into its floral night–
Not yours, not mine, no breeder's and no keeper's,
No homeless walker's, late, no early sleeper's
With bunched unfragrant roses in her room,
Forced from false brightness into curtained gloom.
That rose is not the rose
Which, potted, on a fourth floor balcony shows
One bloom to one who knows
That cash is cash but your cash is not mine:
His tending only made the bought rose shine,
And she for whom he saw it to the hour
When stalk and leaf fulfil themselves, in flower.
Does your tautology
Sprout from a bush or tree,
From any of the ramblers, climbers, creepers?
If less than plastic from a factory,
Metre and rhyme reject what you propose:
Your rose is not a rose is not a rose.

Tony Harrison

A COLD COMING
from 'THE GAZE OF THE GORGON'

'A cold coming we had of it.'
  T.S. Eliot
  JOURNEY OF THE MAGI

I saw the charred Iraqi lean
towards me from bomb-blasted screen,

his windscreen wiper like a pen
ready to write down thoughts for men,

his windscreen wiper like a quill
he's reaching for to make his will.

I saw the charred Iraqi lean
like someone made of Plasticine

as though he'd stopped to ask the way
and this is what I heard him say:

'Don't be afraid I've picked on you
for this exclusive interview.

Isn't it your sort of poet's task
to find words for this frightening mask?

If that gadget that you've got records
words from such scorched vocal chords,

press RECORD before some dog
devours me mid-monologue.'

So I held the shaking microphone
closer to the crumbling bone:

'I read the news of three wise men
who left their sperm in nitrogen,

three foes of ours, three wise Marines
with sample flasks and magazines,

three wise soldiers from Seattle
who banked their sperm before the battle.

Did No.1 say: God be thanked
I've got my precious semen banked.

And No.2: O praise the Lord
my last best shot is safely stored.

And No.3: Praise be to God
I left my wife my frozen wad?

So if their fate was to be gassed
at least they thought their name would last,

and though cold corpses in Kuwait
they could by proxy procreate.

Excuse a skull half roast, half bone
for using such a scornful tone.

It may seem out of all proportion
but I wish I'd taken their precaution.

They seemed the masters of their fate
with wisely jarred ejaculate.

Was it a propaganda coup
to make us think they'd cracked death too,

disinformation to defeat us
with no post-mortem millilitres?

Symbolic billions in reserve
made me, for one, lose heart and nerve.

On Saddam's pay we can't afford
to go and get our semen stored.

Sad to say that such high tech's
uncommon here. We're stuck with sex.

If you can conjure up and stretch
your imagination (and not retch)

the image of me beside my wife
closely clasped creating life...

(I let the unfleshed skull unfold
a story I'd been already told,

and idly tried to calculate
the content of ejaculate:

the sperm in one ejaculation
equals the whole Iraqi nation

times, roughly, let's say, 12.5
though that .5's not now alive.

Let's say the sperms were an amount
so many times the body count,

2,500 times at least
(but let's wait till the toll's released!).

Whichever way Death seems outflanked
by one tube of cold bloblings banked.

Poor bloblings, maybe you've been blessed
with, of all fates possible, the best

according to Sophocles i.e.
'the best of fates is not to be'

a philosophy that's maybe bleak
for any but an ancient Greek

but difficult these days to escape
when spoken to by such a shape.

When you see men brought to such states
who wouldn't want that 'best of fates'

or in the world of Cruise and Scud
not go kryonic if he could,

spared the normal human doom
of having made it through the womb?)

He heard my thoughts and stopped the spool:
'I never thought life futile, fool!

Though all Hell began to drop
I never wanted life to stop.

I was filled with such a yearning
to stay in life as I was burning,

such a longing to be beside
my wife in bed before I died,

and, most, to have engendered there
a child untouched by war's despair.

So press RECORD! I want to reach
the warring nations with my speech.

Don't look away! I know it's hard
to keep regarding one so charred,

so disfigured by unfriendly fire
and think it once burned with desire.

Though fire has flayed off half my features
they once were like my fellow creatures',

till some screen-gazing crop-haired boy
from Iowa or Illinois,

equipped by ingenious technophile
put paid to my paternal smile

and made the face you see today
an armature half-patched with clay,

an icon framed, a looking glass
for devotees of "kicking ass",

a mirror that returns the gaze
of victors on their victory days

and in the end stares out the watcher
who ducks behind his headline: GOTCHA!

or behind the flag-bedecked page 1
of the true to bold-type-setting SUN!

I doubt victorious Greeks let Hector
join their feast as spoiling spectre,

and who'd want to sour the children's joy
in Iowa or Illinois

or ageing mothers overjoyed
to find their babies weren't destroyed?

But cabs beflagged with SUN front pages
don't help peace in future ages.

Stars and Stripes in sticky paws
may sow the seeds for future wars.

Each Union Jack the kids now wave
may lead them later to the grave.

But praise the Lord and raise the banner
(excuse a skull's sarcastic manner!)

Desert Rat and Desert Stormer
without scars and (maybe) trauma,

the semen-bankers are all back
to sire their children in their sack.

With seed sown straight from the sower
dump second-hand spermatozoa!

Lie that you saw me and I smiled
to see the soldier hug his child.

Lie and pretend that I excuse
my bombing by B52s,

pretend I pardon and forgive
that they still do and I don't live,

pretend they have the burnt man's blessing
and then, maybe, I'm spared confessing

that only fire burnt out the shame
of things I'd done in Saddam's name,

the deaths, the torture and the plunder
the black clouds all of us are under.

Say that I'm smiling and excuse
the Scuds we launched against the Jews.

Pretend I've got the imagination
to see the world beyond one nation.

That's your job, poet, to pretend
I want my foe to be my friend.

It's easier to find such words
for this dumb mask like baked dogturds.

So lie and say the charred man smiled
to see the soldier hug his child.

This gaping rictus once made glad
a few old hearts back in Baghdad,

hearts growing older by the minute
as each truck comes without me in it.

I've met you though, and had my say
which you've got taped. Now go away.'

I gazed at him and he gazed back
staring right through me to Iraq.

Facing the way the charred man faced
I saw the frozen phial of waste,

a test-tube frozen in the dark,
crib and Kaaba, sacred Ark,

a pilgrimage of Cross and Crescent
the chilled suspension of the Present.

Rainbows seven shades of black
curved from Kuwait back to Iraq,

and instead of gold the frozen crock's
crammed with Mankind on the rocks,

the congealed geni who won't thaw
until the World renounces War,

cold spunk meticulously jarred
never to be charrer or the charred,

a bottled Bethlehem of this come-
curdling Cruise/Scud-cursed millenium.

I went. I pressed REWIND and PLAY
and I heard the charred man say:

Linton Kwesi Johnson

Mi Revalueshanary Fren

mi revalueshanary fren is nat di same agen
yu know fram wen?
fram di masses shatta silence –
staat fi grumble
fram pawty paramoncy tek a tumble
fram Hungary to Poelan to Romania
fram di cozy cyaasle dem staat fi crumble
wen wi buck-up wananada in a reaznin
mi fren always en up pan di same ting
dis is di sang im love fi sing:

Kaydar e ad to go
Zhivkov e ad to go
Husak e ad to go
Honnicka e ad to go
Chowcheskhu e ad to go
jus like apartied
will av to go

awhile agoh mi fren an mi woz taakin
soh mi seh to im:

wat a way di eart a run nowadays, man
it gettin aadah by di day
fi know whey yu stan
cauz wen yu tink yu deh pan salid dry lan
wen yu teck a stack yu fine yu ina quick-san
yu noh notice ow di lanscape a shiff
is like valcanoe andah it an notn cyaan stap it
cauz tings jusa bubble an a bwoil doun below
strata sepahrate an refole

an wen yu tink yu reach di mountain tap
is a bran-new platow yu goh buck-up

mi revalueshanary fren shake im ed an im sigh
dis woz im reply:

Kaydar e ad to go
Zhivkov e ad to go
Husak e ad to go
Honnicka e ad to go
Chowcheskhu e ad to go
jus like apartied
will av to go

well mi nevah did satisfy wid wat me fren mek reply
an fi get a deepa meanin in di reaznin
mi seh to im:

well awrite
soh Garby gi di people dem glashnas
an it poze di Stallinist dem plenty prablem
soh Garby leggo peristrika pan dem
canfoundin bureacratic strategems
but wi haffi face up to di cole facks
im also open up pandora's bax
yes, people powa jus a showa evry howa
an evrybady claim dem demacratic
but some a wolf an some a sheep
an dat is prablematic
noh tings like dat yu woulda call dialectic?

mi revalueshanary fren pauz awhile an im smile
den im look mi in mi eye an reply:

Kaydar e ad to go
Zhivkov e ad to go
Husak e ad to go
Honnicka e ad to go
Chowcheskhu e ad to go
jus like apartied
will av to go

well mi couldn elabarate
plus it woz gettin kinda late
soh in spite a mi lack af andahstandin
bout di meanin a di changes
in di east fi di wes, nonediless
an alldow mi av mi rezahvaeshans
bout di cansiquenses an implicaeshans
espehshally fi black libahraeshan
to bring di reaznin to a canclueshan
ah ad woz to agree wid mi fren
hopein dat wen wi meet up wance agen
wi coulda av a more fulla canvahsaeshan

soh mi seh to im, yu know wat?
im seh wat? mi seh:

Kaydar e ad to go
Zhivkov e ad to go
Husak e ad to go
Honnicka e ad to go
Chowcheskhu e ad to go
jus like apartied
soon gaan

Alice Keen

A Greyhound in the Evening After a Long
Day of Rain

Two black critical matching crows,
calling a ricochet, eating its answer,

dipped
        home

and a minute later
the ground was a wave and the sky wouldn't float.

                    *

With a task and a rake,
with a clay-slow boot and a yellow mack,
I bolted for shelter under the black strake dripping of timber,

summer of rain, summer of green rain
coming everywhere all day down
through a hole in my foot.

                    *

Listen listen listen listen

                    *

They are returning to the rain's den,
the grey folk, rolling up their veils,
taking the steel taps out of their tips and heels.

Grass lifts, hedge breathes,
rose shakes its hair,
birds bring out all their washed songs,
puddles like long knives flash on the roads.

*

And evening is come with a late sun unloading a silence,
tiny begin-agains dancing on the night's edge.

But what I want to know is
whose is the great grey wicker-limbed hound,
like a stepping on coal, going softly away...

Mimi Khalvati

STONE OF PATIENCE

'In the old days,' she explained to a grandchild bred in England,
'in the old days in Persia, it was the custom to have a stone,
a special stone you would choose from a rosebed, or a goat-patch,
a stone of your own to talk to, tell your troubles to,
a stone we called, as they now call me, a stone of patience.'

No therapists then to field a question with another,
but stones from dust where ladies' fingers, cucumbers
curled in sun. Were the ones they used for gherkins
babies that would have grown, like piano tunes had we known
the bass beyond the first few bars? Or miniatures?

Some things I'm content to guess: colour in a calyx-tip,
is it gold or mauve? A girl or a boy... Patience
was so simple then: waiting for the clematis to open,
to purple on a wall; the bud to shoot out stamens,
the jet of milk to leave its rim like honey

on the bee's fur. But patience when the cave is sealed,
a boulder at the door, is riled by the scent of hyacinth
in the blue behind the stone: the willow by the pool
where once she sat to trim a beard with kitchen scissors,
to tilt her hat at smiles, at sleep, at congratulations.

And a woman, faced with a lover grabbing for his shoes
when women-friends would have put themselves in hers,
no longer knows what's virtuous. Will anger shift
the boulder, buy her freedom, and the earth's? Or patience,
like the earth's, be abused? Even nonchalance

can lead to courage, to conception: a voice that says
oh come on darling, it'll be all right, oh do let's.
How many children were born from words such as these?
I know my own were; now learning to repeat them, to outgrow
a mother's awe of consequences her body bears.

So now that midsummer, changing shape, has brought in
another season, the grape becoming raisin, hinting
in a nip at the sweetness of a clutch, one fast upon another;
now that the breeze is raising sighs from sheets
as she tries to learn again, this time for herself.

to fling caution to the winds like colour in a woman's skirt
or to borrow patience from the stones in her own backyard
where fruit still hangs on someone else's branch... don't ask her
whose? as if it mattered. Say: *they won't mind*
as you reach for a leaf, for the branch, and pull it down.

Michael Laskey

A Late Wedding Anniversary Poem

Knowing time's short in the rush
hour of breakfasts with children to crush
into coats and partings to brush

I tucked your second best bra
in over the radiator

so that hurrying to dress
you might almost feel me press
a warm hand around each breast.

John Levett

A Shrunken Head

He's been stitched-up; two gummed, black-threaded eyes
Squint back across the decades in surprise
Through spiteful chinks of sunlight, acrid smoke,
Screwed-up against some wicked tribal joke.
His rictus has been sewn into a smile,
A tight-lipped dandy, puckered into style,
The clearing where his grisly fame began
Still broods beneath the kinks of wood-stained tan.
Flayed leather now, his features smoked and cured,
His niche in culture gruesomely secured,
The needled grin is fixed, drawn back and set
Bone-dry in its reflective cabinet.
A hundred years ago he strayed alone
Towards this room of ritual skin and bone,
Believed in spirits, drank, was secretive
With knives and fish-hooks, dreamed his seed would live,
Sheathed his penis, sweated half the night
On invocations, prayed, prepared to fight,
And felt, perhaps, the moon's leaf-parted shine
Move up his legs and bathe his severed spine;
His head hacked off, half-baked into this face
That swings and grins inside its airless case.
Hung-up, he seems to twitch at each dropped word,
As if, although we whisper, he had heard,
And stares through us to what we cannot see,
Our unstitched smiles, their pale atrocity.

David Lightfoot

TURNING POINT

They say that after twenty-five
our bodies cease to grow and then begin
to die. It is, though we're alive,
the unsignposted fount and origin
of our inevitable slide
towards that pot-hole which awaits us all –
the time bricklaying genes decide
they've built enough and let their trowels fall.

Their break, though only seconds long,
is sensed by some – those of a cast of mind
described as mystical, those song –
or poem-scribblers – as the time to find
the mortal man suspended there
just like a spinning coin before it fails
and guess from glimpsing, if they dare,
if that poised life will come down heads or tails.

But are the men themselves aware
that it has come, this moment when the genes
are programmed simply to repair?
Do they know what this brief hiatus means?
Perhaps in retrospect it now
explains those *frissons*, sudden stabs of fear
which in the prime of life somehow
make all our structured certainties unclear.

Michael Longley

Detour

I want my funeral to include this detour
Down the single street of a small market town,
On either side of the procession such names
As Philbin, O'Malley, MacNamara, Keane.
A reverent pause to let a herd of milkers pass
Will bring me face to face with grubby parsnips,
Cauliflowers that glitter after a sunshower,
Then hay rakes, broom handles, gas cylinders.
Reflected in the slow sequence of shop windows
I shall be part of the action when his wife
Draining the potatoes into a steamy sink
Calls to the butcher to get ready for dinner
And the publican descends to change a barrel.
From behind the one locked door for miles around
I shall prolong a detailed conversation
With the man in the concrete telephone kiosk
About where my funeral might be going next.

Lachlan MacKinnon

THE SINGLE LIFE

The aquarium in the Chinese take-away
bumps the noses of gross, bulb-headed fish whose eyes plead
for the excellence of their trapped souls like postulant
anorexics floundering in fatness. They mouth
and mouth but cannot reproduce the costive
knowing vowels of girls at tables in the restaurant
with their assured, imperious 'You eat that this way',
nuzzling the bottom for missed feed, expertly spitting gravel.

I wait over a glass of white wine. Through plastic strips
masking a door, smells drift and a television
shows me some muddy water and a dead tree
trying to drown. The rains have come and gone
like a net curtain when the breeze turns.
Lions assemble at the water, giving
each other the odd sideways high-table glance.
A snake swallows a frog. The legs stop moving.

Mary Maher

By-Pass

At the time we laughed
and trivialised our way
through it. February.
Sometimes fingers flutter
over his chest.

He lay that day
on a high bed,
limbs stretched;
pinned like dead
play.

I counted them.
Nine tubes,
wires, going into
coming out
of him.

And kind uniformed persons just had time
to put his sponged hand in mine. Soft.
And continued rallyng round and round
him. And me, a slipway of their route.

I pushed my stool close
to the steel leg tube
of his bed.
I did not want to get in their way.
Just his.

And then in a breather they discussed
what they were going to have for dinner.
Our life that day was a day in their lives.
That surgeon! He must live numerously
on the broken edge of other people's crises.
The pace! I saw him fourteen days running
in those corridors.

This summer at the back of the house
my man builds dry stone walls
with quarried stone.
Near the house he finds a broken land drain
which bleeds and bleeds into the far corner of the room.
Distraught he digs down to the cracked earthenware,
replaces it with plastic pipes
that bend.

Glyn Maxwell

WE BILLION CHEERED

We billion cheered.
  Some threat sank in the news and disappeared.
It did because
  Currencies danced and we forgot what it was.

It rose again.
  It rose and slid towards our shore and when
It got to it,
  It laced it like a telegram. We lit

Regular fires,
  But missed it oozing along irregular wires
Towards the Smoke.
  We missed it elbowing into the harmless joke

Or dreams of our
  Loves asleep in the cots where the dolls are.
We missed it how
  You miss an o'clock passing and miss now.

We missed it where
  You miss my writing of this and I miss you there.
We missed it through
  Our eyes, lenses, screen and angle of view.

We missed it though
  It specified where it was going to go,
And when it does,
  The missing ones are ten to one to be us.

We line the shore,
> Speak of the waving dead of a waving war.
And clap a man
> For an unveiled familiar new plan.

Don't forget.
> Nothing will start that hasn't started yet.
Don't forget
> It, its friend, its foe and its opposite.

Medbh McGuckian

A Different Same

Moonlight is the clearest eye:
Moonlight as you know enlarges everything.
It occupies a pool so naturally
It might have grown there.
Its stoniness makes stones look less than us.
Our hands begin to feel like hooves
Deep in this life and not in any other.
It can free the crossed arms from the body
Where time has fitted them without question,
And place them once random in a swimming
Position, so it seems you have opened
Without sound. There are figures standing
On steps, and figures reading. Not one
Walks past without being blurred
Like bronze snapshots. The church bell hangs
In the swirling porthole of the yew tree,
Pierced by a sea as abstract and tough
As the infant around the next corner.
Morning, mid-morning, afternoon and evening,
The rose that is like a pink satin theatre
Programme spreads to three gardens
With her roots in one. Her gaze, from the intersection
Of the terrace, gathers in the horizon,
A ceiling of translucent planes
With paintings of fruit in each. Awake at night
Uprooted me from some last minute shoulder.
I came out of the photograph
With that year underneath this dream;
It met with his mouth.

Jamie McKendrick

Il tremoto

Inside the mountain earth begins to move
its joints and spring the links that pegged it down
– the fans of schist, the chocks and wedges of

feldspar and chert. A daylight owl screws back
from rock that spilling derelicts her nest
then quiet plugs the ear, a twist of wax.

Behind the quiet a core of silence hums
until earth moves again – this time in earnest:
dumb matter's rigid-tongued delirium

wrung at the verge of the crack that gapes at
the heart of things, that widens the Norman watchtower
from its sunken gateway to the parapet

as the tide uncoils. This means in Purgatory
a soul pinned to the rock has broken free

Ian McMillan

Snails on the West Shore, August 1991

It had been raining, and my son
wanted to see the snails. We ran
out of the guesthouse, long before breakfast,

our feet brushing the owner's Telegraph
in the hall where the paperboy had left it,
almost stepped on the face of John McCarthy,

blinking in the light of the world's flash
and we ran towards the Gogarth Abbey Hotel
where Alice Liddel stayed as a little girl,

Alice in Wonderland waiting inside her
like the idea of a butterfly waits inside
a picture of a caterpillar. My son

did his usual trick, running like mad
at a gang of gulls, laughing as they
climbed the sky, landed on the roof

of the Gogarth Abbey Hotel. Then we began
to see the snails, far more than yesterday,
dozens of them, punctuating the damp path

like they owned it, slowly, so slowly,
from the wall to the road. My son
stopped, his three-year-old head

focussing down to the snails moving slow
as the low clouds that hung over the Orme.
He stared at the snails, the slow old man

inside him waiting like the idea of a bird
waits inside a picture of an egg. Down past
the Gogarth Abbey Hotel a gull swooped down

on a snail, bashed it on the floor, rose
towards the Orme's clouds and the grey sky.
My son was frightened, looked down

at the snails crossing the path, looked up
at the gulls slicing the sky's silence, looked
at me, saw the boy I once was, the slow

old man I would become, crossing paths
in a grey winter. Later, in the residents'
lounge, he laid his cars out in a long line;

"Is it a traffic jam?" I asked. "It's snails
crossing the path" he said. I bent down
to pick one of the cars up. "Leave it"

he said, "It's a snail crossing the path."
I looked up, saw John McCarthy on the TV,
blinking in the light of the world's flash,

thought of how we must learn to live together;
snails, young boys, fathers, and the slow
old men they must become, under the Great Orme

and the clouds dark as a cell door.

Patrick Moran

In Memory of Frank Neville

His verses rarely stirred divining rods,
And never found the ease of trampolines:
Yet he wore poetry like a habit.

Each night, his heart beating to word and rhyme,
He'd strain beyond grease and skins, the crushed butts,
The single bed: all for a dream of wings

That led, finally, to his own backyard...
His coat and glasses folded on the rim
Of the dark tank they fished his body from.

David Morley

Ozymandias To You

I

A poet stayed a month in my half made building:
a trellis of iron, my hopeless skyscraper-to-be.
  The poet liked girders, said they were line endings.
He said they were the line endings of Vladimir Mayakovsky.
  He took the room above the liftshaft and he loved the echoes,
        echoes were second nature.

I told him of my cement mixers, two years in coming
and look, damn it, at all this Industrial Sand.
  He said, useless, Egyptian, and went about in shorts.
It was a murderous summer, he said,
  a crucial time to be planning any restructuring
        or poems in couplets.

Leave it to Nature, he said. I did. I hopped it
and left the building site open to the weather.
  One big storm and my site became Sudan,
an overnight fairground for all the local children.
  They had never seen my sea, the tide was always out
        somewhere, out there.

The tide was always out and the sands were of my making.
Oh, employees lorried in from satellite villages!
  How you picnicked with vodka, your wives and girls,
hatched natterjacks under my corrugated iron,
  belched incorrigibly, made love by the brick piles.
        Roman love, the real thing.

They liked me for allowing it and came to me singing.
I was suddenly famous for all the wrong reasons.
  All the wrong reasons were rightly too tempting.
The poet wrote my eulogy or was it an elegy?
  He lifted it from the *Collected* of Percy Bysshe Shelley,
            a Party Man apparently.

He said their folksy traditions and late night stories
were resurrecting in the sands. My sands, I mean.
  Well, there was certainly something: madrigals, rhapsodies.
There were certainly candles, all night blow-outs,
    the colossal wreck of bonfires in the morning,
                their strange, charred hearts.

II

When the police finally raided I hoiked up a megaphone.
They thought it was a blunderbus, lobbed the CS gas in.
  The poet caught it in the face but was lucky;
it was just one of his many masks, the one marked *Posterity*.
  He made shift with ten other masks he threw to the children
            with appropriate instructions.

He said the Architecture of Realism was a fixed route up Vesuvius.
That the police were the sherpas, the coolies, the carriers.
  Our position in Time was sufficient to justify,
well, expeditions into anything, if it led to lucidity.
  He said he would write us up (this was above our heads)
            by charring every word.

He said other things beside, not all of them clear.
We took up with the singing though there wasn't any choice.
  So I showed them the blueprint the moment we were finishing
and tore it before them and h a n d e d it to the police.
  We took a while to vanish, but the process was starting
            from the first white tear

and continued ███████████ ████ ████ ██████████,
████████████ ██ ██████ through history
███████████████ ██████ until a smear of snow ████
████ like a slick of ███████████ ████████ ███████
████████████████ semen was all that
            remained of us.

Thom Nairn

A Quiet Business

We could watch the rattled cavalcade
Winding
In and through
Slippery mist
Far below.

Torches, the wandering truck lights
Snagging on harsh lands,
Mirrored from stark rock.

Here, direction becomes
As irrelevance
Only the bats and snakes
Comprehend.

Sometimes,
Our eyes above cloud,
Identified seas,
            wandering sands
            mountains
Which could not exist:

And always
Half way into something
Approaching night.

A heat and light too,
Strangely
As present as ice,
Though its opposite.

This is a Dreamtime
Far from the terse, anarchic
Awareness of the ice.

Watching the rattled cavalcade
And no distant voices,
Some movements
Are a quiet business:

Just the torches,
The reflection of truck lights
On our collecting tins,

And knowing only the sound,
The far off bumping,
Of a loose
Dinosaur thigh bone
In the bottom of a trailer.

(I am indebted to Kerr Yule here, his tss,
THE FELLOWSHIP OF HUMANKIND,
provided the kick off point for
this poem and I have adapted, appropriated
and "borrowed" material directly
from Kerr's own collaging and constructions
from a mass of diverse works).

Sean O'Brien

PROPAGANDA

After the whole abandoned stretch,
The bricked-up arches, flooded birchwoods,
The miniature oxbows and dubious schools,
After the B-roads that curved out of sight
Beneath bridges to similar views,
All the scenery hauled away backwards
While this train was heading elsewhere,
After the threat to our faith in the railways,
It seems that at last we have come to the place
That described us before we were thought of.
We stand on its sweltering, porterless platform
And wait in the time-honoured manner.
The stalled afternoon's like a story
Once left on a train with a chapter to go,
Smelling of oil, of dust and old sunlight.
Here are the canopy, flowertubs, posters for war
And the bum-frying torpor of benches.
Here are the smoke in the throat of the tunnel,
The footbridge a guess in the glare, and the clank
As the points irreversibly switch, and here
Is the perfect assurance that somewhere
Close by it is quietly happening.

It's here that Germany in person calls
By parachute, at first confused to death
By Brough and Slough, by classroom spinsters
Jumping on the hand-grenades. Their dull reports
Alert the author sleeping at his desk,
The curate and the mower in the fields.
A bucket fills and overflows, abandoned
To blacken the stones of a whitewashed yard.
In the brown upper rooms there are women
Attending to letters. We are not permitted
To stand at their shoulders and may not
Determine the date, but the subject
Is things going on as they must, the summer
Still adding fresh months to itself, and the way
You'd never guess by simply looking round.

How easy to know where we stand, within sight
Of the back-to-front fingerpost, certain
That commandeered railings still rust
In the sidings, that somewhere up there
In the ferns is what looks like a gate
But is really a lock on the gelid
Forgotten canal, that its waters retain
All their monochrome heat and exist
For the drenching of constables.
O Mr Porter, the convicts are coming,
Ineptly, their suits full of arrows,
Over the dismal, bunkered levels,
Still sawing their irons and shouting.

It's midnight. On schedule, the ghost train
Is failing the bend by the claypits,
And stiff with old service revolvers,
Unsleeping on hard wooden chairs –
The price of this unnecessary trip –
We stare at the waiting-room fireplace and know
That the corpse in its bundle of coats
Will awake and the door be flung open
When Hammerpond enters, no longer a tramp,
To deliver the long explanation
Whose end we will miss when the radio coughs
And announces that all roads are flooded,
The sovereign's in Canada, Hitler in Brighton,
And no one will leave here tonight.

Bernard O'Donoghue

A NUN TAKES THE VEIL

That morning early I ran through briars
To catch the calves that were bound for market.
I stopped the once, to watch the sun
Rising over Doolin across the water.

The calves were tethered outside the house
While I had my breakfast: the last one at home
For forty years. I had what I wanted (they said
I could), so we'd loaf bread and Marie biscuits.

We strung the calves behind the boat,
Me keeping clear to protect my style:
Confirmation suit and my patent sandals.
But I trailed my fingers in the cool green water,

Watching the puffins driving homeward
To their nests on Aran. On the Galway mainland
I tiptoed clear of the cow-dunged slipway
And watched my brothers heaving the calves

As they lost their footing. We went in a trap,
Myself and my mother, and I said goodbye
To my father then. The last I saw of him
Was a hat and jacket and a salley stick,

Driving cattle to Ballyvaughan.
He died (they told me) in the country home,
Asking to see me. But that was later:
As we trotted on through the morning mist,

I saw a car for the first time ever,
Hardly seeing it before it vanished.
I couldn't believe it, and I stood up looking
To where I could hear its noise departing

But it was only a glimpse. That night in the convent
The sisters spoilt me, but I couldn't forget
The morning's vision, and I fell asleep
With the engine humming through the open window.

Michael O'Neill

LOST

After Benediction hot drinks then bed,
the moon rising from the monstrance of a cloud.

*

Venice. Years on. And years ago. We doubled back
and missed our way and came upon a square

shuttered and sun-struck, with a dead-end look.
A pack of stray cats baked.

*

Candles. Candles and worn eyes. And the words:
'Tower of Ivory... Queen of Peace'.

*

Tonight the moon is full, a systematic white;
you're in the dark or at any rate lost,

or caught for ever in that moment by a window,
or on a vaporetto heading for the island of the dead.

*

'Lost', you say, liking the sound. Also 'candles',
'years', 'Venice', 'monstrance'. And then again 'lost'.

Evangeline Paterson

LUCIFER AT THE FAIR

Blowing my last bob
on the Jungle Ride, I saw him.
Tawny and lithe as a hunting
cat, he balanced and swayed
on the racketing heave of the boards.
I whirled like an atom around him

to thunderous music. He took
my shilling, gazing aloof,
while I, thin as a lizard,
with skinned knees, went bucketing
past, uncoveted prize in my
striped school dress. If he'd spoken
a word to me, I'd have died.

For hours I lay, seeing,
printed on night, him
glow like a dark angel
at the heart of his whirring planet.

Pauline Plummer

UNCLES AND AUNTIES

I was afraid of uncles,
with laughs like football crowds,
wearing bark coloured clothes,
taking up more space than allowed.

They smelt of cities and work.
Shirts could not contain
the bristles sprouting through collars
and cuffs, the fingers nicotine stained.

A man exposed himself
to me when I was just a kid.
Impossible to tell anyone of his revolting
pinkness, what his flapping trousers hid.

No wonder I preferred aunties –
in their flowery dresses, scrub rough hands,
faces dusted with icing sugar,
permanently permed; lips, strawberry jammed.

Peter Porter

WITTGENSTEIN'S DREAM

I had taken my boat out on the fiord,
I get so dreadfully morose at five,
I went in and put Nature on my hatstand
And considered the Sinking of the Eveninglands
And laughed at what translation may contrive
And worked at mathematics and was bored.

There was fire above, the sun in its descent,
There were letters there whose words seemed scarcely cooked,
There was speech and decency and utter terror,
In twice four hundred pages just one error
In everything I ever wrote – I looked
In meaning for whatever wasn't meant.

Some amateur was killing Schubert dead,
Some of the pains the English force on me,
Somewhere with cow-bells Austria exists,
But then I saw the gods pin up their lists
But was not on them – we live stupidly
But are redeemed by what cannot be said.

Perhaps a language has been made which works,
Perhaps it's tension in the cinema,
Perhaps 'perhaps' is an inventive word,
A sort of self-intending thing, a bird,
A problem for an architect, a star,
A plan to save Vienna from the Turks.

After dinner I read myself to sleep,
After which I dreamt the Eastern Front
After an exchange of howitzers,
The Angel of Death was taking what was hers,
The finger missed me but the guns still grunt
The syntax of the real, the rules they keep.

And then I woke in my own corner bed
And turned away and cried into the wall
And cursed the world which Mozart had to leave.
I heard a voice which told me not to grieve,
I heard myself. 'Tell them', I said to all,
'I've had a wonderful life. I'm dead.'

Peter Reading

from EVAGATORY

Forest, Sarawak, limestone outcrop,
caverns of roosting Bornean horseshoe bats
(faeces of which are sifted by cockroaches);

one-and-a-half miles into the labyrinth,
   reservoir, stalactitic vaulting,
etiolated, eyeless crustacean,
         wheeze of a Tilley lamp near expiry.

         Guideless, directionless, lightless, silence.

                    *

Edge of black Baltic, night, north-easter,
         low-ceilinged candle-lit gloomy *keller*,
flocculent-headed yeast-fragrant beer, a bench,
         basins of pork-dripping, coarse sour rye-bread,
         Germanic drone of a drunk salt's slurred dirge,
whisper of scented soft-breathed translationese:

Mine is a sea-borne sorrowful history,
   winters of toil through tempests, foam frosts,
   fearing the future's vicious voyage,
   lashing of iced brine, hurled hail, waves' thrash,
longing for land and cuckoo's sad call of spring...

         nothing on earth can abide forever,
         illness or age or aggression takes us,
         striving for fame beyond death is futile
(none will be left to celebrate heroes' *lof*).

days and delights depart, and inferior
            beings infest and despoil earth, each one
    greys and grows grave and, pallid, passes.

            ...dawn of each day I bewail my sorrows,
            how I was sundered in youth from homelands

(fuelled by a yeast-frothed litre, a wandering
            dosser drones on in the local lingo),

no man grows wise without many winters spent
            pondering folly of worthless world's-gear,

awful the apprehension of earth-ending,
            crumbled the mead-hall, no laugh lasting,

where are the heroes, word-hoarders, feasting-feats? –
gone back to dark as though they had never been,

life is a loan and bank accounts transient,
            kindred are skewered on sharp-spiked ash-spears,

            all of this world will be Weird-wreaked,
                                            emptied...

                        *

            Province of hyperborean bleakness,
            Cranium. Roused by nightmare (in which
    I am a butcher, cleaver repeatedly
        hacking your carcass, five-years-dead friend),
    grief gushes raw again from an old lesion.

Christopher Reid

AMPHIBIOLOGY

Like old men frolicking in sacks
seals slither on the sea-thrashed rocks.

Why does their melancholy sport
exert such a strong pull on my heart?

I could stand here for hours on end
watching them fail to make dry land.

From time to time one gains brief purchase,
adopting the pose of a Grand Duchess.

In seconds, though, a fist of surf
rises to swipe the pretender off.

Repetitive slapstick, it has the charm
of earliest documentary film.

Stuffed statesmen and wind-up warriors
turn to salute us across the years...

Only, in this case, something far
more ancient seems to hang in the air.

It could be the question, whether to plump
for a great evolutionary jump

or stay put in the icy brine.
May the good Lord send them a hopeful sign!

Mark Roper

SKINDEEP

After my bath I put on
your red dressing gown.

It unnerved me. It smelt
so strongly of you.

In a lampshade of flesh
I was haunting, haunted.

Reading Levi you'd asked
if I thought

I could have survived
one of the Camps.

But women were destroyed
immediately and how

should my thin skin survive
the loss of yours?

A vacuum salesman once
drew from our mattress

deposits
of a soft grey talc.

Silt of our spent skins,
mingled, inextricable.

Image of perfect union.
Then he showed us

blown-up photos
of the bugs that thrive

on such leavings.
No phoenix rises

from the rub of two skins
no matter how urgently

how often they kindle
and feast on what lies

between them. The wolf
in sheep's clothing

that spirits one of us
away will leave the other

fleeced, hidebound,
plumbing skindepth.

William Scammell

THE EMPEROR OF CHINA
after Heine

My father was a dry old stick,
a martyr to angina
but me, I wet my lips, and I'm
the Emperor of China.

It has green fingers, my sweet schnapps,
it sows a wild perfume
and when I look into my mind
all China is in bloom!

The swamps dry out, the peasants turn
to happy nymphs and gentle swains.
One glance from me, my wife swells up
melodiously with labour pains.

The sick take up their beds and walk.
The civil service goes to work.
All error dies. Peace takes root.
The PM budgets on his flute.

Asparagus instead of rice
is what my people eat.
The pingpong fans dance on the green
by two and two, with nimble feet.

And palace mandarins file out
to smile a meum, tuum,
pigtails flying roundabout
the Heavenly Bicycle Museum.

All the temples fill with souls,
with incense, and with prophecies;
bandits take up begging bowls;
the Jews convert, on bended knees.

Then all the bigwigs vote themselves
out of a job, for love of China.
Rule over us, you poets, rule
flat out, like Heinrich Heine!

*

I drink too much, the doctor says.
Much he knows, of words or wine.
Here's a health, a Marseillaise
in mandarin. This empire' s mine!

Jo Shapcott

PHRASE BOOK

I'm standing here inside my skin,
which will do for a Human Remains Pouch
for the moment. Look down there (up here).
Quickly. Slowly. This is my front room

where I'm lost in the action, live from a war,
on screen. I am an Englishwoman, I don't understand you,
What's the matter? You are right. You are wrong.
Things are going well (badly). Am I disturbing you?

TV is showing bliss as taught to pilots:
Blend, Low silhouette, Irregular shape, Small,
Secluded. (Please write it down. Please speak slowly.)
Bliss is how it was in this very room

when I raised my body to his mouth,
when he even balanced me in the air,
or at least I thought so and yes the pilots say
yes they have caught it through the Side-Looking

Airborne Radar, and through the J-Stars.
I am expecting a gentleman (a young gentleman,
two gentlemen, some gentlemen). Please send him
(them) up at once. This is really beautiful.

Yes they have seen us, the pilots in the Kill Box
on their screens, and played the routine for
getting us Stealthed, that is, Cleansed, to you and me,
Taken Out. They know how to move into a single room

like that, to send in with Pinpoint Accuracy, a hundred
Harms.
I have two cases and a cardboard box. There is another
bag there. I cannot open my case – look out,
the lock is broken. Have I done enough?

Bliss the pilots say is for evasion
and escape. What's love in all this debris?
Just one person pounding another into dust,
into dust. I do not know the word for it yet.

Where is the British consulate? Please explain.
What does it mean? What must I do? Where
can I find? What have I done? I have done
nothing. Let me pass please. I am an Englishwoman.

Jon Silkin

Urban Grasses

With a sickle, I tended the dead in London
shortening the grass that had flowered
on their bodies, as it had in my child's.
And I piled the soil over the paupers' flesh
in their flimsy coffins, which split. What else
was I to do? It became
my trade, my living.

*

Earth, I shall be unhappy to not know
how you go on, when I'm like those
I tended, shearing the grasses
above their foreheads. I felt tenderness
yet I did not know them – and how should I re-assure
that nothing, and say, yes, I care for you
because you are nothing now. Yet you are nothing.
Could I have dared tell them?
and therefore I remained silent.

Harry Smart

FLORINS

Let's keep a place in the digital
Decimal world for an honest word like *florin*.
So much more solid and satisfying
Than *ten pee piece*, so much more
Suggestive of that thickly silver disc,
Hard, yet rubbed to congeniality
With flesh, smooth in the hand.
Florins, a handful of florins,
A man could be happy with a handful of florins.

Tonight I walked home through the town
With three florins tucked comfortably
Between my knuckles, just in case.

Stephen Smith

Beside Lough Neagh

The lough's peaty intestines throw back
no mirror image of the sky.
The lough's dark centre sucks the sunlight
in like a black star. Here my fathers

worked the linen crops in 17,
weaving khaki blankets for the troops,
till 'flax-lung' bandaged up their breaths
The climate's perfect with its yeasty air

for moistening the brittle cloth.
As kids we used to dive in there.
Now I think Sodom and Gomorrah
could be sunk under its depths.

a localised apocalypse,
rating small mention in the world at large.
I imagined Belfast going down on fire.
Here, water's a secret metaphor:

Priests sign a symbol on your head
at birth. Transparent and indelible,
it still feels chilly on my brow;
water washes free the gun-man's tracks

from earth. Though Belfast's sunk beneath
its weight, there are mariners
under my blood, who surface now and then
to breathe. They push my accent into grief.

Pauline Stainer

from THE ICE-PILOT SPEAKS

St. Brendan's monks
sail through the eye
of the iceberg.

At first, they ran
with the shadow of the land
through light bluish fog

later, by moonlight,
the ship caulked
with tallow, shamans

clashing over the Pole
as if to earth
any dead in the rigging,

and at dawn,
floes gliding by,
chesspieces in lenten veils

the sea a silver-stained
histology slide,
the O of the iceberg

whistling like Chinese birds
with porcelain whistles
on their feet.

Even in prayer
they could never replay it–
the purity of that zero

Varèse, playing
the density of his flute's
own platinum

the intervening angel
bearing a consignment
of freshwater.

Matthew Sweeney

Asleep in a Chair

Asleep in a chair for three hours?
Take that man away. Bind him
and bundle him into a mini-cab,
drive through the Southern English night
till you see the lights of Brighton,
then throw him out on the South Downs.

Hopefully it will be sub zero
and wet as Ireland. (*Drunk* and
asleep in a chair for three hours,
with the TV and the gas fire on?)
Pick a field with cattle in it,
or better still, a nervy horse.

Make sure there's no stream near,
or even a house. Get miles away
from a shop or a chemist –
empty out his pockets just in case.
Smash his glasses while you're at it.
Forget you liked him, lose his name.

Burn his shoes to ash beside him,
keep his jeans as a souvenir.
Cut his hair off (*all* his hair).
Asleep in a chair for three hours?
By the time you've finished, honey,
he might have learned to sleep in a bed.

Charles Thomson

RAMSGATE IN THE RAIN

We saved our Persil coupons
  and from Maidstone caught a train
to spend the day beside the sea
  at Ramsgate, in the rain.

We took our lunch in a café
  and we took up smoking again
and we took a stroll for souvenirs
  from Ramsgate, in the rain.

We went into the amusement arcade
  where the videos addle the brain,
and we looked at the little harbour
  of Ramsgate, in the rain.

It was really rather romantic,
  though the sky was a great grey stain,
to spend last Sunday with you
  in Ramsgate, in the rain.